ALL ABOUT PROFESSIONAL FOOTBALL

Running Pro Football

Commissioner, Owners, Front Office, and More

by Ted Brock

ALL ABOUT PROFESSIONAL FOOTBALL

Running Pro Football: Commissioners, Owners, Front Office, and More

by Ted Brock

Huntington City Township
Public Library
255 West Park Drive
Huntington, IN 46750
www.huntingtonpub.lib.in.us

Mason Crest
450 Parkway Drive, Suite D
Broomall, PA 19008
www.masoncrest.com

Printed and bound in the United States of America.

Series ISBN: 978-1-4222-3576-8
Hardback ISBN: 978-1-4222-3585-0
EBook ISBN: 978-1-4222-8308-0

First printing
1 3 5 7 9 8 6 4 2

Produced by Shoreline Publishing Group LLC
Santa Barbara, California
Editorial Director: James Buckley Jr.
Designer: Bill Madrid
Production: Sandy Gordon
www.shorelinepublishing.com

Cover photograph by Matt Dunham/AP Photo.

Library of Congress Cataloging-in-Publication Data is on file with the Publisher.

CONTENTS

Key Icons to Look For

Words to Understand: These words with their easy-to-understand definitions will increase the reader's understanding of the text, while building vocabulary skills.

Sidebars: This boxed material within the main text allows readers to build knowledge, gain insights, explore possibilities, and broaden their perspectives by weaving together additional information to provide realistic and holistic perspectives.

Educational Videos: Readers can view videos by scanning our QR codes, providing them with additional educational content to supplement the text. Examples include news coverage, moments in history, speeches, iconic sports moments, and much more!

Text-Dependent Questions: These questions send the reader back to the text for more careful attention to the evidence presented here.

Research Projects: Readers are pointed toward areas of further inquiry connected to each chapter. Suggestions are provided for projects that encourage deeper research and analysis.

Series Glossary of Key Terms: This back-of-the-book glossary contains terminology used throughout this series. Words found here increase the reader's ability to read and comprehend higher-level books and articles in this field.

INTRODUCTION

Without the people who built the NFL and continue to fuel its growth, the players wouldn't be the big stars they are today.

32 = 1

By just about any measure, the National Football League is America's—and perhaps the world's—most popular sports league. With revenues of $13 billion in 2015 and a solid place atop opinion polls as "favorite sport," the NFL is an enormous success.

That it continues to grow is a testament to nearly 100 years of vision, ambition, and discipline. The men who formed the league in 1920 were unable to throw in the $100 their own rules said they owed. So they sealed their agreement with a handshake.

Early NFL leaders built the framework that kept the league alive through the Great Depression and World War II. The era of television launched pro football on its dizzying ride. And now, in the digital age, detailed information hits hard and often.

The people who built and continue to build the NFL are the subject of this book. This is a picture of pro football's key figures then and now—from the commissioner to the league office to the 32 teams. They know their product. They understand its power. They never stop making it grow.

CHAPTER 1

A Pennsylvania football club paid Pudge Heffelfinger $500 to play for its team, making him the first official pro player.

Forming the League

Today, the NFL landscape glitters with money and fame. Its players are icons, its team logos **adorn** every possible product, and its teams rake in money. The origins of this huge enterprise are much more humble, however. Here's a brief look at how the NFL was formed and how those beginnings—and some key steps along the way—continue to have a huge impact on the sport today.

The first college football game was played in 1869. The game's popularity spread from the colleges to private athletic clubs in Ohio and Pennsylvania. In 1892, American football got its first professional player. William Walter "Pudge" Heffelfinger received $500 to play one game.

Words to Understand

adorn to decorate

chaotic completely confused or disordered

tainted dishonored or discredited

A swarm of pro football teams dotted the map for the next 20 years. Most of them struggled financially. Scheduling was **chaotic**. Teams bid against each other for top talent, while the game itself was brutal and disorganized. Players earned two- and three-figure amounts per game. College players assumed false identities to earn extra bucks on Sundays. It was time to all start working from the same playbook.

Birth of the League

In August of 1920, representatives of four pro teams met in a Canton, Ohio, automobile showroom. They formed the American Professional Football Conference. A month later, 10 more teams joined the group. It was renamed American Professional Football Association, then became the National Football League in 1922.

During the 1920s and 1930s, NFL teams came and went, among them one-year wonders such as the Tonawanda Kardex (0–1 in 1922), the Kenosha Maroons (0–4–1 in 1924), and the Kansas City Cowboys (8–3, the NFL's fourth-best record, in 1926).

The original 14 franchises in 1920 swelled to 22 in 1926. The stock market crash of 1929 and the Great Depression both took a toll, as many teams ran out of money and/or fans. By 1932, the NFL was down to eight teams.

Two teams joined the following year, and the NFL split into Western and Eastern divisions. (Of course, back then "Western" was a bit of a reach. Chicago was the farthest west NFL team until the Los Angeles Rams joined in 1951.) In the first official NFL Championship Game, the Chicago Bears defeated the New York Giants, 23–21, for the 1933 title.

After World War II, the new All-America Football Conference (1946–49) began as a rival to the NFL. The AAFC expanded the sport's reach to the West Coast with the Los Angeles Dons and San Francisco 49ers. In 1950, the AAFC and the NFL merged. Three teams from the AAFC—

Look Who's Back

In January 2016, Los Angeles again became an NFL city when owners voted to approve the St. Louis Rams' move to Inglewood, an L.A. suburb. Pro football had left town in 1995—the Rams for St. Louis and the Raiders heading back to Oakland after 13 years in L.A.

The Rams' winning plan had to overcome a rival bid by the Raiders and the San Diego Chargers. They proposed sharing a new stadium in Carson, another L.A. suburb. The owners' vote wasn't a total loss for the Chargers. They were given the option of coming to L.A.; if they opted out, the Raiders could negotiate with the Rams.

the 49ers, Cleveland Browns and Baltimore Colts—became part of a 13-team NFL.

That reformed new league began appearing on national television for the first time in 1956, as TV took the country by storm. In 1958, the league's national championship game changed the future of both the medium and the sport.

On December 25, 1958, the Baltimore Colts and New York Giants played the NFL Championship Game at the Polo Grounds in New York City. The first 60 minutes were not an artistic success. The last eight-and-a-half minutes changed NFL history. A 17–17 tie after four quarters forced a new term into the language of pro football: sudden-death overtime.

The Colts took the ball and went 80 yards in 13 plays to win 23–17. But the outcome that mattered was the marriage of television and the NFL: the drama of Baltimore quarterback Johnny Unitas masterfully directing his team's winning drive, finishing with Alan Ameche's touchdown from one yard out. One game suddenly generated a new level of suspense and enjoyment…and ratings.

Network television executives woke up Monday morning hungry for more. NFL executives suddenly understood their product as never before. It would prove to be a perfect marriage between sport and media. The game's three-hour length, its hori-

zontal field (just like a TV set), and its hard-hitting action (with plenty of time for commercials) all added up to TV gold. Thanks to TV, pro football over the next six decades would dominate the sports media landscape in the United States. Rights fees would rise from around $20 million to more than $1 billion a year.

Intense love of the game by guys like these has turned the NFL on TV into a huge revenue source.

Another Rival Forces Change

Another newcomer to pro football, the eight-team American Football League (AFL), joined the national sporting scene in 1960, threatening the NFL's growing popularity.

Inside the NFL-AFL merger

TV money got real in this decade, too. In 1964, the NFL signed a two-year deal with CBS for $28.2 million. The AFL was in the fifth and last year of a deal with ABC worth over $2 million a year. The AFL then switched to NBC, which paid $36 million for five years.

In 1966, the NFL and AFL agreed to merge in 1970, but to have the league champions meet at the end of the season right away. The first AFL-NFL World Championship Game was played at the Los Angeles Memorial Coliseum on Jan. 15, 1967. Green Bay of the NFL defeated Kansas City of the AFL 35–10. The Packers beat the Oakland Raiders the following year.

The annual championship game eventually changed its name to the Super Bowl—a monicker it lived up to in January 1969. "Broadway Joe" Namath, the AFL New York Jets quarterback, boldly predicted a victory in Super Bowl III over the heavily favored Baltimore Colts of the NFL. The Jets won 16–7. The Super Bowl has since become America's number-one sporting event.

In 1970 the AFL-NFL merger took full effect. Twenty-six teams shared a then-staggering $142 million in TV rights fees paid by the three major networks. CBS mainly carried the NFC. NBC mainly carried the AFC. And ABC introduced *Monday Night Football*.

Share and Share Alike

League-wide corporate sponsorships became more and more common. NFL Properties was formed in 1962 to manage the league's marketing, licensing, and publishing divisions. Meanwhile, NFL Films cranked out miles of game and feature footage and became world-renowned. For all these ventures, and the all-important TV money, the NFL established a business relationship among its teams that continues to help make it successful. All money earned by the league as a whole—as opposed to money that a particular team gets from tickets or local radio, etc.—is divided equally among all 32 teams. That means a team in Green Bay, Wisconsin, a city of a little more than 100,000 people, gets just as much national money as one in the New York area, with its tens of millions of fans. This, more than any one thing, has made the NFL thrive.

As the 1970s went on, pro football overtook baseball as America's favorite sport. Television revenues grew rapidly over the next five decades. The game got faster. Players became more specialized.

Over that time, certain players' individual expression brought rules against taunting, showboating, and violating the NFL uniform code. Illegal substances, including performance-enhancing drugs, posed disciplinary problems for the league. In the Internet age, the NFL's media footprint grew slowly at first, then gained speed after 2000 with the arrival of NFL.com and, later, NFL Network. A nine-year package of broadcast contracts began in 2014, worth a staggering $28 billion. Compare that to the tens of millions brought in by TV in the 1960s. Super Bowl XLIX in February of 2015 was the most-watched TV program of all time.

A decade and a half into the 21st century, the NFL's prosperity was **tainted** by two issues. One was an alarming increase in serious, often criminal, player misconduct. The other was equally alarming: a rise in traumatic brain injuries, many of them life threatening, among former players. On the eve of pro football's second century, the face in the NFL's mirror was an image of celebration and concern.

 # Text-Dependent Questions

1. Who was the first player in America to be paid to play football?

2. What team won the 1958 NFL Championship Game in sudden-death overtime?

3. What does NFL Films do for the league?

 # Research Project

Look up a video of the 1958 NFL Championship Game. Then watch some current NFL footage. See if you can list 10 major differences between the NFL today and in 1958—how the game was played, what the players wore, or how the game was described.

CHAPTER 2

Commissioner Roger Goodell enjoys a perk of his job: getting to hold the Vince Lombardi Trophy earned by the NFL champion.

THE COMMISSIONER

In November of 2015, HBO interviewed President Barack Obama. He was asked whether he might become a sports commissioner when he left office.

"Well, I'm best suited for basketball," Obama said, "but I cannot believe that the commissioner of football gets paid $44 million a year." He added that NFL teams were "...making a profit, and I think that's what the owners are most concerned with."

Words to Understand

abruptly suddenly

dementia severe impairment or loss of intellectual capacity and personality integration, due to the loss of, or damage to, neurons in the brain

discretion freedom of judgment or choice

lobbied tried to convince politicians to support a cause

meteoric extremely rapid and often unexpected

nullify to render or declare legally void or inoperative

parity equality, as in amount, status, or character

publicist media expert who helps companies and products get their message to the public

That $44 million figure was for 2012; it was "down" to $34 million in 2015. *The New York Times* noted that commissioner Roger Goodell "...helped steer the league through a legal minefield. In August [2013], the NFL agreed to pay $765 million to settle lawsuits brought by about 5,000 retired players who accused the league of hiding the dangers of concussions. Some analysts believe the deal could have been for far more." In other words, Goodell might have saved the owners more than what he made in salary.

As the leader of the biggest sports league in the nation, Goodell is sought for autographs just like his players are.

As a measure of the NFL's power and profitability, compare Goodell's pay to what commissioners in other sports receive. Major League Baseball commissioner Rob Manfred's salary is not officially revealed, but was widely estimated at $20 million. National Hockey League Commissioner Gary Bettman made $8.3 million in 2012, the last year official figures are available. News media estimates say former National Basketball Association Commissioner David Stern made as much as $23 million. The NBA does not reveal the official figure. Clearly, even at the top, the NFL is king.

He Has 32 Bosses

The NFL commissioner serves at the pleasure of the owners. Officially, he is not their boss...they are his. Never mind that the last NFL commissioner to be removed by the owners was Elmer Layden in 1946.

The NFL commissioner's job description is a long one. It takes up 11 pages in the league's constitution and by-laws. Here is a highly condensed version:

- He is "a person of unquestioned integrity," elected by a two-thirds vote of NFL owners. They also determine the length of his service and how much he is paid.
- He has the power to judge disputes between and/or among owners, clubs, coaches, players, officials, and other NFL employees.
- He has "sole **discretion**" over expenses he decides are appropriate.
- He presides over negotiations for broadcast and television rights fees.
- He negotiates with other businesses and other associations.
- His disciplinary powers include suspending and banning coaches, players, officials, and officers working for the NFL.

It's a very demanding, difficult, and high-profile job. Though the pay is tremendous, so is the pressure and the amount of responsibility. Since the NFL began, only eight men have held this high office. In fact, only five of them have been called Commissioner; the job was NFL President from 1920–1941.

The Men in the Hot Seat

Here's a look at all the No. 1 leaders in NFL history.

Jim Thorpe (1920)

More than football: Jim Thorpe, greatest athlete ever?

Thorpe, a Native American, was the country's first true football superstar—a college halfback with speed and power. His professional career began with the Canton (Ohio) Bulldogs in 1915 and lasted 14 years. Thorpe played with seven teams and would become a member of the Pro Football Hall of Fame's charter class in 1963. He was chosen as the first league president, but his role was mostly ceremonial or on the field. He played nearly the full season for the Bulldogs, then led the team to New York City for a game at the Polo Grounds that drew 20,000 spectators. Thorpe's name recognition earned the new league a ton of exposure and respect.

Joe Carr (1921–1939)

Stability was Carr's immense contribution. He had been a club owner (Columbus Panhandles), and

Carr's experience as a team owner helped him understand what his fellow owners needed.

proved he could endure the NFL's growing pains.

Carr introduced a league constitution and by-laws. Teams received territorial rights to players. Official schedules and standings appeared for the first time. In 1925, NFL teams agreed to a standard player contract. Carr also improved relations between pro football and the more popular college game. In 1925 he approved a rule that kept NFL teams from hiring a college player before his class had graduated. Carr also recruited owners whose finances were solid, and moved nine of the 10 NFL teams to major cities.

Carl Storck (1939–1941)

Storck had a short, quirky time as leader of the NFL. He was named president when Carr died. In 1941, NFL owners established a commissioner as a separate office. The owners voted Elmer Layden to the position and kept Storck in the role of president. But Storck **abruptly** resigned. He said he did it "for the best interests of the game." Stock had been with the NFL for 20 years, 15 as a volunteer.

Elmer Layden (1941–1946)

Layden had been a famous college player in the 1920s as part of a Notre Dame backfield named for "The Four Horsemen," the biblical messengers of the world's end. By the time World War II was over, Layden's disapproval among league owners meant his NFL days were numbered. From the beginning, some owners complained that all franchises had not taken part in selecting him. Time ran out on Layden when Brooklyn owner Dan Topping moved his Dodgers to the new All-America Football Conference. Owners felt the gentlemanly Layden hadn't fought hard enough to keep the team. He resigned in early 1946.

Bert Bell (1946–1959)

Bell had been a co-founder of the Philadelphia Eagles in 1933. In 1946, he was co-owner of the Pittsburgh Steelers. He sold his interest in the Steelers, then moved NFL headquarters to a suburb of Philadel-

Bell's time as the commissioner saw a large expansion of the league and its first jump into TV.

phia. In 1950, Bell merged the NFL and the All-America Football Conference. He also took on the Canadian Football League over scheduling conflicts and player rights.

Bell saw that the Los Angeles Rams' attendance figures had suffered from their having televised all their home games in 1950. It appeared that fans were staying at home to watch instead of going to the games in person. Bell became a fan of the "blackout rule," which later would become official NFL policy. To promote attendance, fans within a 75-mile (120 km) radius would be unable to receive a local team's televised game.

The NFL always has loved pointing out the **parity** among its teams. But it was Bert Bell who came up with the expression, "On any given Sunday, any team can beat any other team." He died in 1959 at Philadelphia's Franklin Field while attending a game between the Eagles and Steelers, his two former teams. NFL treasurer Austin Gunsel served as president in the office of the commissioner until January of 1960.

Pete Rozelle (1960–1989)

Rozelle had been general manager of the Los Angeles Rams since 1957. Prior to that he had been a sports **publicist** at Compton College and the University of San Francisco. His public relations and management skills brought future riches to the NFL and its teams.

Rozelle's vision helped turn the NFL from a pro sports league to an entertainment giant.

Rozelle aggressively **lobbied** Congress to pass the Broadcast Act of 1961, and President John F. Kennedy signed the bill into law. It enabled the NFL to do two things: one, sign a contract limiting NFL telecasts to one network; and two, share the revenues equally among all NFL teams. In 1960, the newly formed American Football League already had installed

revenue sharing among its teams. Rozelle followed the AFL's lead.

The merger agreement between the AFL and the NFL put Rozelle in charge of the new 26-team NFL in 1970. Regular season and Super Bowl TV revenues launched a skyrocketing annual payday for every franchise. The league already had begun spinning off companies such as NFL Films and NFL Properties. And corporate sponsors in the Rozelle Era soon began displaying the NFL shield, for which they paid increasingly huge amounts.

Three areas of distress clouded Rozelle's last decade as commissioner: drug scandals involving cocaine and steroid use among players; labor issues that led to a shortened 1982 season; and franchise shifts—Oakland Raiders owner Al Davis' move to Los Angeles in 1982 and Baltimore Colts owner Robert Irsay's middle-of-the-night getaway to Indianapolis in 1984. Rozelle spearheaded a long legal battle to **nullify** the Raiders' move. The Raiders won the case.

When Rozelle retired, the NFL had grown to 28 teams. Television revenues had risen to nearly $500 million a year. The NFL's current status, size, income, and reach all trace their roots to Rozelle's leadership.

Paul Tagliabue (1989–2006)

Tagliabue was a lawyer who had represented the NFL in court. Some people cringed at the thought of a non-football man in the commissioner's chair. A number of owners wanted co-commissioners—one would be a football veteran, the other would be an expert on business and legal issues.

Tagliabue brought a legal background to the job that helped with labor talks with the players.

During Tagliabue's time in office, the NFL added expansion franchises in Carolina, Jacksonville, and Houston, plus a new Browns' franchise in Cleveland, to swell the league roster to 32 clubs.

Tagliabue had moments of social consciousness: He moved Super Bowl XXVII from Phoenix to Pasadena because the state of Arizona refused to make Martin Luther King Jr.'s birthday a state holiday. In 2001, Tagliabue canceled all games scheduled for the week-end following the September 11 terrorist attacks. He also gets credit for reaching out to women and Latinos and for creating an NFL youth fitness program.

In 1994, concussions among NFL players were on the rise. Tagliabue downplayed the problem, calling it a "pack-journalism issue." He said the rate was "one concussion every three or four games," which amounted to 2.5 concussions for every "22,000 players engaged." Two decades later and beyond, the "pack-journalism issue" had become a plague on the sport.

NFL Network joined America's cable TV lineup while Tagliabue was the commissioner. Meanwhile, broadcast rights fees soared into the billions. Relations between the league and the players were generally good, and Tagliabue could point to 17 years without a players' strike.

Roger Goodell (2006–present)

More than any other NFL commissioner, Goodell has struggled in the public eye. He came straight from the league office, where he had served as chief operating officer. His term saw a **meteoric** rise in broadcast revenue and a financial position that dwarfed every American sport.

Two serious issues clouded Goodell's first 10 years: head injuries leading to early **dementia** and death among former NFL players, and current players' violent behavior off the field. In 2015, the film *Concussion* addressed the NFL's medical nightmare: the discovery of chronic traumatic encephalopathy (CTE), a massively destructive brain disease found among former NFL players.

Goodell's handling of incidents involving Baltimore Ravens running back Ray Rice nearly cost the commissioner his job in 2014. A video surfaced showing Rice dragging his unconscious fiancée out of an elevator. After five months, Goodell suspended Rice for two games. A month later, an apologetic Goodell published a stricter domestic abuse policy. A week after that, a new video showed Rice punching his wife

Owners at Work

The 32 club owners make up the NFL Executive Committee, a kind of commissioner's "cabinet." Since 2011 its chair has been New York Giants President and CEO John Mara.

The NFL Executive Committee has several smaller committees that deal with specific league functions: Broadcast, Business Ventures, Competition (rules and on-field issues), Digital Media, Finance, Hall of Fame, Health and Safety Advisory, International, Investment, Labor, Legislative, NFL Network, Stadium, Stadium Security and Fan Conduct, Super Bowl, and Workplace Diversity.

Goodell calls for more women to have key roles in NFL

in the elevator. The NFL suspended him indefinitely.

As the stories of these varied men have shown, the role of the NFL commissioner has grown tremendously since Jim Thorpe did it on a part-time basis. While the man who holds the job wields enormous power, he is held back by having to make 32 team owners happy, as well as try to appease players seeking more money and influence and safety, as well as tens of millions of fans of the game. It's not exactly a thankless job, but it probably has more headaches than joy.

Of course, he does not work alone. A massive NFL headquarters staff of experts in various fields all report to him and his top associates. We'll meet several of them in the next chapter.

The NFL is not a corporation like Nike or Apple, which exist to make money for their shareholders. But as the person in charge of the NFL, the commissioner is very much like a chief executive officer. And like a good CEO, he always gets great seats to the game.

Text-Dependent Questions

1. What superstar player was the league's first president?

2. Why was the Broadcast Act of 1961 important to the NFL?

3. What did Commissioner Paul Tagliabue call a "pack-journalism issue?"

Research Project

Choose any four of the eight commissioners in the NFL's first century. Imagine all of them are alive. Write a scene of dialogue among the four men at the location of your choice—having dinner, on a walk, maybe even watching pro football. The topic of conversation: What has become of the NFL?

CHAPTER 3

TAMP

Many fans have never heard of him, but Tim Leiweke, the NFL's chief operating officer, plays a big role in running the league.

THE LEAGUE OFFICE

The NFL games we watch on Sundays in the fall are packed with competitive drama. During the work week, in a tall building on New York's Park Avenue, billions of dollars are at stake.

The commissioner can't handle it all. His support staff is small, if you count only the league's other "officers": the secretary and treasurer. And each of the two conferences has a president.

The commissioner leans heavily on experts—from cyber-security technicians to medical researchers to digital media. For instance, commissioner Roger Goodell and NFL Media head Brian Rolapp meet for a week each year with companies in California's Silicon Valley. From

Words to Understand

integrity honesty

intellectual property information, ideas, logos, and any material produced by human beings that can be copyrighted and controlled

plaintiffs in a legal case, the parties bringing the action to the court

those meetings come strategies such as Yahoo!'s first-ever live streaming of a regular-season game in 2015. Each major decision goes through a pathway of experts before the commissioner makes the final decision—or asks the owners to vote on a decision.

Key Officials

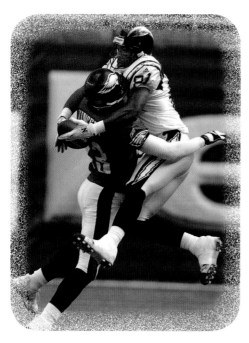

Troy Vincent (in green) has moved from the playing field to the NFL office as a key executive.

Four key executives sit below Goodell on the NFL Inc. chart. The names are the office holders as of March 2016, but the duties of their offices remain even if new people are hired.

Chief operating officer Todd Leiweke joined the NFL in July 2015 to fill Goodell's old job, which had been vacant since Goodell was promoted to commissioner in 2006. Goodell was swamped with player conduct issues and choosing a team to play in Los Angeles. Enter Leiweke, who had been chief executive of the National Hockey League's Tampa Bay Lightning and before that chief executive of the Seattle Seahawks. The COO of the NFL co-ordinates the running of the league office, and also spearheads key projects such as team movement.

Senior vice president of football operations Dave Gardi was hired in March 2014 after being part of the league's legal team since 2003. He represented the league and its teams in collective bargaining agree-ments with the NFL Players Association, and had worked on issues such as officiating, rules, and player discipline. His position focuses on the game on the field, plus related issues such as travel, scheduling, and rules. The football operations department makes sure the game itself remains…at the top of its game!

Executive vice president of football operations Troy Vincent played cornerback with the Miami Dol-phins and Philadelphia Eagles from 1982 to 1988. Vincent ran the NFL Player Engagement Program from 2010 to 2014. His executive role includes offi-ciating, on-field discipline, and game operations. This job, often held by former players, is the hands-on, day-to-day organizer of the football operations staff. The senior vice president is more of an officer, while the executive vice president is in the field, meeting with teams and players.

Chief content officer Jordan Levin became the first to occupy his job in June 2015. He had been executive vice president at Xbox Entertainment Studios. He oversees NFL Network, the NFL Now online platform, and other properties owned by the league. He also is in charge of the Super Bowl Halftime Show. Many sports leagues and major companies now have content officers, whose job includes just about any way that the league is presented to the public. In the NFL's case, that job focuses on media that the league controls, not necessarily the broadcast of games on networks other than NFL Network. NFL content reaches tens of millions of people each week with an enormous variety of offerings; this officer coordinates all that work.

The Legal Team

The NFL has to constantly be aware of protecting itself legally. The men and women of the legal department negotiate television rights fees, sponsorship contracts, and labor contracts . . . for starters.

In 2016, the NFL had 23 attorneys in its legal department. At the top is the NFL's vice president of legal affairs, who since 2013 has been Anastasia Danias, an expert in **intellectual**

property law. Her office handles contracts between the players' union and the NFL, as well as contracts among league sponsors. The office also helps individual teams with legal issues regarding NFL marks and logos, plus defends the league against any lawsuits. The biggest one of those in recent years was filed by retired players regarding head injuries suffered while playing.

One of the jobs of the legal team, led by Danias, is making sure Super Bowl tickets are not counterfeited.

"The 6,085 **plaintiffs** [among them, 3,973 former players] are basically claiming that the NFL knew or should have known of what they claim are long-term cognitive risks of repeated head injuries, and that the NFL either hid those risks or didn't do enough to prevent them," Danias said. "We vigorously dispute those claims."

As head injuries increase, the NFL's moral dilemma—and the work of its busy legal department—grows more intense: How can a sport whose entertainment value depends on violent collisions continue to thrive?

Selling the League

The NFL has three main sources of income: television rights fees, team income, and NFL Ventures, Inc.

Some stores have added branded NFL sections, especially during big events such as the Super Bowl.

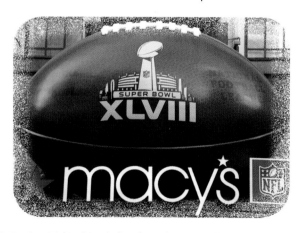

NFL Ventures, which includes four smaller divisions, accounts for almost a quarter of the league's revenues each year. One of them, NFL Enterprises, is responsible for advertising, publicizing, promoting, marketing, and selling broadcasts of NFL games. Another division is in charge of selling league-wide sponsorships—such as the "official beer" or "official pizza" of the NFL—which in 2015 reached $1.5 billion.

NFL Enterprises also includes NFL.com. The website is the official source for NFL news, video highlights, fantasy football, and game-day coverage. It features NFL Now, a treasury of game highlights and short features. NFL.com also is a platform for "Play 60," the league's youth fitness program. It began as "Play Football" under commissioner Paul Tagliabue.

Another division, NFL Properties, works on licensing and marketing of team-owned trademarks and logos. Companies submit bids to NFLP in hopes of being allowed to display the NFL shield on their products. Companies that win such bids pay huge sums of money to the NFL for the rights to put that famous shield—or team logos—on everything imaginable—hats, jackets, shirts, picnic coolers, refrigerator magnets…and hundreds more. NFL Properties was formed in the early 1960s as the first of the league's many revenue-sharing projects. It has become the model for all of the "32 = 1" revenue generated by the league.

NFL Productions is a video service that produces NFL-related programming for the league and its teams. Its main focus is on NFL Network and NFL Films. In 2003, the league started its own cable network, NFL Network. While basically competing with the networks that pay the NFL billions, the network gives the league a place where it controls the content and keeps all the revenue. Since 2012, for instance, it has carried live prime-time Thursday-night telecasts.

NFL International deals with marketing, publicizing, promoting, licensing, distributing, and developing the NFL's international business. The NFL has its eye on someday perhaps adding a London franchise. Already, three games each season are played there. Mexico City is another NFL haven; in 2016 a regular-season game was held there. Increasing sales of licensed products internationally reflect the strength of the NFL brand.

The Officials

Without on-field officials—the people in the striped shirts—there is no NFL. The **integrity** of the game means everything. Ask tens of millions of fans. Think about billions of dollars.

Like any NFL season, 2015 had its share of controversial calls. A touchdown catch by Detroit Lions receiver Golden Tate became a flashpoint. Media outlets analyzed it to death. Commissioner Goodell even appointed a "catch committee." The controversy again raised the possibility of making NFL officials full-time employees. Right now, they work only on weekends during the season, while devoting evening hours to study and meetings, but most hold other full-time jobs.

Will technology replace all the on-field officials someday?

NFL vice president of officiating Dean Blandino runs the NFL office that trains, hires, and supervises its officials. He knows a star player's comments can fuel public outrage over the way a key game is officiated.

Possible officials from all levels of football are judged by NFL scouts and executives, first on film and then in development programs. Selected candidates attend offi-

NFL officials are actually part-time workers. Most hold down a "regular" job the rest of the week.

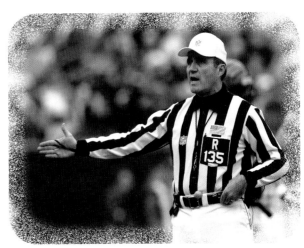

Voice of God

NFL Films began telling the story of the league to the world more than five decades ago. Films began when Ed Sabol, his son Steve, and four others filmed the 1962 champion-ship game between the Giants and the Packers. They hired Philadelphia newscaster John Facenda, whose deep style was dubbed "The Voice of God," as their narrator. A typical sequence: The ball spiraling in flight against an empty sky. The crowd suddenly visible in the background as the ball descends and then settles into a receiver's outstretched hands. Their work and techniques have become standard practice in sports broadcasting.

ciating clinics. Their first assignments are training camps and preseason games. The process takes from two to three years.

Ten new officials worked NFL regular-season games in 2015. For the first time in league history, a woman was part of that group, as former college official Sarah Thomas was hired as a line judge.

All officials are evaluated on an individual and group basis. Under-performing crews can be reassigned from high-profile to lower-profile games. Individual officials can be dis-missed for poor performances.

Planning Rules Changes

NFL.com notes that rules changes make the game "fairer, safer, and more entertaining." The eight-member NFL

Competition Committee, made up of owners and coaches, recommends rules changes. Then all 32 owners vote on whether to adopt them.

"What is good about the committee is the opportunity to sit in a room and [discuss] ideas over and over again," said Atlanta Falcons president and CEO Rich McKay, chairman of the committee. The discussion is thorough. The committee reaches out to coaches, the players' union, officials, medical experts, and others. Video, statistics, injury reports, and other resources come into play.

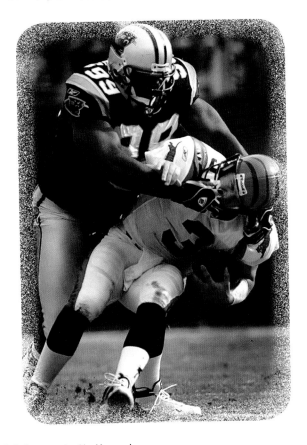

Pulling the facemask, as shown here, has long been a penalty, but new rules about player safety are always being considered.

What prompts a rule change? Common sources include controversies over plays or players, unusual circumstances, and trends in scoring and injuries.

Rules against targeting, grabbing the facemask, horse-collar tackling, and tackling while leading with the helmet have all been addressed recently. They are all aimed at improving player safety. Still, the number of concussions among NFL players in 2015 rose dramatically. Was that because of increased focus on detecting them? Or on more hard hits by players? Or a combination?

Rules can also be changed for non-safety reasons. In 2015, the point-after-touchdown kick was moved from the 2-yard line to the 15-yard line to increase its difficulty. The move worked as previously nearly perfect kickers missed key PATs, adding suspense to many games. The committee will continue studying the game and is certainly not afraid of making changes to the rules.

The Season Schedule

A small division of the operations staff has a big job. Each year, it has to create a complete, 17-week regular season schedule. Each year, each team plays 16 games in 17 weeks, with one week off as a "bye." Each team plays the other three clubs in its division twice—home and away. Each division also matches up against another division on a rotation basis. But then the math and the organization get really tricky.

Schedulers have to take long trips into account. A West Coast team shouldn't have back-to-back cross-country flights. What about the teams playing in London? Those teams need a week off after those games for jet lag. Then there are TV concerns, with an eye to creating the biggest ratings for national broadcasts. Which match-ups will work best on *Sunday Night Football*, the NFL's marquee game of the week? Monday- and Thursday-night games can leave teams with a short recovery time, so those have to be spaced out.

Creating the NFL's entire schedule is a complex job that starts the minute the previous season ends and involves weeks of computer work and hours of meetings and talks. Every team will have input, but no one team will get everything it wants. In the end, it always seems to work out, though!

Labor Talks

The commissioner and the NFL legal team are key players in negotiations between the league and the NFL Players Association (NFLPA). The NFLPA is the union to which all players belong, and it negotiates on their behalf. Each player has an individual contract with a team, but all those contracts have to include language agreed to by the NFL and NFLPA regarding all players. Sometimes, the discussions about that language can lead to problems.

In 2011, talks aimed at reaching a collective bargaining agreement came to a halt. An agreement reached in 1993 had been renewed four times. Now the league wanted a larger share of revenue. The players resisted. With no resolution in sight, the NFL locked out players from teams' facilities and shut down league operations from March 12 to July 25. Both sides took significant legal action during the four-month standoff. Finally a new collective bargaining agreement was reached. The agreement's main areas of concern were free agency, the salary cap, rookie salaries, minimum salaries, and teams' right to place a "franchise" or "transition" tag on a player to retain his rights. The agreement expires in 2021.

 # Text-Dependent Questions

1. Explain the importance of the NFL's legal team.

2. What are the NFL's three main sources of income?

3. Name three ways the NFL uses its "nerve center."

 # Research Project

Research how often teams asked for a review of a play on the field, and how often the teams were right (and the officials were wrong). Has the number of overturned calls changed from year to year?

CHAPTER 4

Chris Grier took over as the Miami Dolphins general manager in 2016. First stop, the press conference to tell fans his plans.

THE FRONT OFFICE

Each of the NFL's 32 teams has its own structure. Unlike a company, an NFL team is not run by shareholders or directors. In fact, a league rule says a company can't own a team, but must be owned or at least controlled by a single person or family. (The Green Bay Packers are an exception, as we'll see.)

A team's management style depends on its owner. Three basic models have evolved since pro football began. The most common puts power mainly in the hands of the general manager, the president, or a combination of the two. An example of an all-powerful general manager was the lovably grouchy, brilliant George Young, who ran the New York Giants from 1979 to 1997.

Words to Understand

free agents pro sports players not currently signed to a contract

vagabond having an uncertain or irregular course or direction

The Exception

Thirty-one of the NFL's 32 teams are privately owned. The Green Bay Packers are the only publicly held franchise in the league.

The Packers have been an NFL team since 1921. Earl (Curly) Lambeau bought the Packers in 1922. A pile of debt nearly put the franchise out of business. The Packers survived by becoming a nonprofit organization. Citizens of the Green Bay area bought shares in the team. That shared ownership has remained, even as the NFL has grown and changed.

The Packers are governed by a seven-member executive committee, which is elected by a 45-member board of directors. Stockholders (there are more than 360,000) can attend annual meetings, vote for directors, and buy special stockholders-only merchandise—but do not receive income from their investment. Instead, that money goes to the Green Bay Packers Foundation, a charitable organization founded in 1986.

Today, Green Bay (population: 104,000) has the smallest market of any NFL team. The Packers' season-ticket waiting list (just below 100,000) is among the longest in professional sports, with an average wait time of more than 30 years.

An owner occasionally puts the head coach in charge. Philadelphia owner Jeffrey Lurie gave Chip Kelly full control over personnel decisions when he hired him in 2013. Kelly won a division title that year, but was let go before the last game of the 2015 season.

A third model has the owner calling the shots. Dallas Cowboys owner Jerry Jones defines this approach. Jones is as comfortable discussing the play of Cowboys quarterback Tony Romo as he is brokering a stadium deal. Washington Redskins owner Daniel Snyder has angered fans with a highly visible, micro-managing style since buying the team in 1999 for $800 million.

Whatever model an owner goes by trickles down to the staff that runs the team. Most teams, however, have a similar structure of executives and departments. It's common to find former players working as coaches or in the front office, which is the general term for a sport's team's executives.

The Executive Office

An NFL team's president, sometimes called chief executive officer or chairman, runs the finances and reports directly to the owner. He is responsible for marketing, advertising, travel, ticket prices, stadium maintenance, and payroll.

As in many large corporations, the business structure is in the hands of the chief financial officer (CFO). In 2012, the San Francisco 49ers named Cipora Herman, formerly a top Facebook executive, as the first female CFO in NFL history. Like other NFL team CFOs, Herman manages a range of areas: finance, legal, human resources, information technology, and community relations. In 2013 she led the team that secured long-term financing for the 49ers' new home, Levi's Stadium.

Every NFL team has a strong public relations presence in its home city and region. Its media relations staff provides news outlets with access and information—anything from setting up a radio interview to publishing weekly statistical updates. And on game day, the details multiply: last-minute injury updates, the press box seating chart, and post-game interviews, plus heaps of media information during the game.

A team's website, Twitter account, Facebook page and Instagram account obviously are a vital part of presenting the franchise in a positive light. The league dictates certain guidelines, such as a common home page design. But a team's skill with content is what draws eyeballs. The media team is responsible for that.

Many teams have large community relations departments, too, that coordinate charity work and team functions in its local area. They arrange player appearances, visits to hospitals, and donations of team gear.

Each team has groups of people who sell tickets and sponsorships, too. NFL teams are allowed to sell their marks to local groups, as long as they don't conflict with national sponsors, generally. Teams also usually have local radio deals to broadcast their games, often in multiple languages.

Team community events departments arrange for players to make appearances and sign autographs.

The Football People

The general manager runs each NFL team's personnel department, which manages the actual roster of players. He reports directly to the team owner.

The GM has the final say on all decisions that involve players—for example, scouting, draft decisions, signing contracts, and disciplinary measures.

He hires the head coach and the rest of the personnel staff.

Many general managers are former directors of player personnel. This is a key job title at most teams, and is focused on the pro players. Some recent examples include San Diego's Tom Telesco, Cleveland's Michael Lombardi, and Tampa Bay's Mark Dominik. The DOPP negotiates contracts with the team's current players and **free agents.** He also coordinates scouts who evaluate other teams' players.

The director of college scouting also works for the GM. His group of scouts rates players at all levels of the college game. Their communication with college coaching staffs helps measure a player's work habits and other signs that point to success as a pro.

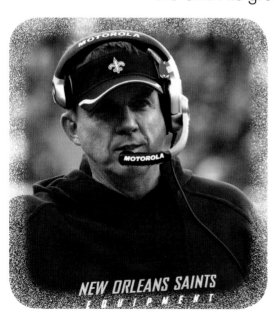

Sean Payton took over as coach of the New Orleans Saints in 2006, making him one of the longest-serving current head coaches.

The Coaching Staff

NFL wisdom: A head coach's first job is coaching his coaches. "Being on the same page" with that staff determines how a team trains and performs. Converting a head coach's philosophy to success on the field is the job of the offensive or defensive coordinator. Each coordinator directs assistant coaches in charge of specific position players. A secondary coach, for example, might have two assistants below him, one for cornerbacks, one for safeties.

It's not uncommon to find NFL teams with two dozen or so assistant coaches. It is uncommon to find a team with exactly a dozen. That would be the Pittsburgh Steelers, old school all the way with the smallest coaching staff in the league. Steelers assistants cover the same basic areas as all teams: offensive and defensive coordinators, quarterbacks, running backs, wide receivers, tight ends, offensive and defensive lines, inside linebackers, outside linebackers, defensive backs, and special teams. Strangely, the Steelers list no strength and conditioning coach. The Super Bowl 50-champion Denver Broncos have three. The Carolina Panthers have an "assistant special teams/nickel backs" coach. The Baltimore Ravens have a "kicking consultant."

Along with hands-on coaches for players, many teams now have large departments for statistical research, using the latest computer analysis to find better players and new ways to win. The Houston Texans have a "director of football research." The Kansas City Chiefs list a "spread game analyst/special projects." The Detroit Lions have "offensive assistant/research and analysis."

In 2016, the Buffalo Bills named Kathryn Smith their special teams quality control coach. She is the NFL's first full-time female coach. Bills co-owner Kim Pegula said, "While we understand the significance of this announcement, it's important to understand that Kathryn earned this position because she has shown she is qualified, dedicated, and puts in the work needed for this role."

Behind the Scenes

Before the players take the field to play, hundreds of people have worked hard to get them, the stadium, and the team's staff ready for the game. The equipment manager and his team of assistants organize

One Team's Coaching Staff

"NFL assistant coach" is hard to define. Each head coach has his own idea of the support he needs. Assistant coaches rarely spend many years with the same team. When a head coach is fired or leaves for a better offer, he often takes many of his assistants with him.

Another rule of the road in this **vagabond** profession: if the group of players you coach begins underperforming, you might be on the road again. And whatever team hires you next, you'd better be flexible: This season's wide receivers coach with team X could easily be next season's cornerbacks coach with team Y.

In 2015, the Seattle Seahawks listed an NFL-high 25 assistant coaches. Below are the men who back up Seahawks head coach Pete Carroll, who was hired in 2010.

Michael Barrow, linebackers
Darrell Bevell, offensive coordinator
Dwaine Board, assistant defensive line
Tom Cable, assistant head coach/offensive line (pictured)
Dave Canales, wide receivers
Chris Carlisle, head strength and conditioning
Brennan Carroll, assistant offensive line
Nate Carroll, assistant wide receivers
Chris Cash, assistant secondary/cornerbacks
Andre Curtis, assistant secondary/safeties
Mondray Gee, assistant strength and conditioning
John Glenn, quality control/defense
Will Harriger, assistant quarterbacks/quality control offense
Travis Jones, defensive line
Pat McPherson, tight ends
Chad Morton, assistant special teams
Kris Richard, defensive coordinator
Pat Ruel, assistant offensive line
Brian Schneider, special teams coordinator
Rocky Seto, assistant head coach/defense
Carl Smith, quarterbacks
Sherman Smith, running backs
Nick Sorensen, assistant special teams
Lofa Tatupu, assistant linebackers
Jamie Yanchar, assistant strength and conditioning

uniforms and every piece of gear, at home and on the road. The information technology staff makes sure all internal and external lines of communication are functioning perfectly, including headsets used by coaches and players during the game. The video staff tracks every moving image in a game or practice and prepares hours of video for the team to review. The training staff and medical doctors, along with nutritionists and sports psychologists, are responsible for preventing and healing injuries and keeping players healthy and fit. And that's not even to mention the many stadium workers—some of whom work for the team while others are employed by the facility—that make sure every aspect of an NFL game works.

Game day is a work day for trainers. They help players stretch and prepare for the game, and they deal with injuries during the contest.

Indeed, countless hours of work go into making sure you enjoy every minute of your favorite team's game. The men and women in the National Football League office—along with those in each club's front office—are mostly invisible to the public. But the work they do makes the very visible work of NFL players happen . . . and it probably couldn't happen without them.

 Text-Dependent Questions

1. Some NFL teams use other titles instead of "president." What are some of those titles?

2. On an NFL team, who is in charge of choosing the pro players?

3. What NFL team has the smallest coaching staff?

 Research Project

Download *The Official NFL Record & Fact Book*. (It's free.) Look up one team's coaching staff biographies. Now print out a map of the United States. Use different-colored markers to draw the career paths of some of the coaches by drawing straight lines from city to city. What patterns do you notice?

Find Out More

Books

2016 Official NFL Record & Fact Book. NFL, 2016.

Carroll, Bob, with Michael Gershman, David Neft, and John Thorn (editors). *Total Football II.* New York: HarperCollins, 1999.

Websites

www.espn.com/nfl
The most visited of all sports websites, this has long been a mainstay in the sports online information lineup.

www.nfl.com
The official site of the National Football League includes a page on the commissioner and lists all league officials. Hit the "Teams" drop-down menu for franchise front office information.

Bonus: Who are the NFL's best team owners?

SERIES GLOSSARY OF KEY TERMS

alma mater the school that someone attended

analytics in sports, using and evaluating data beyond traditional game statistics to predict a player's future success

brass a slang term for the high-ranking executives of an organization

bundling in television, the concept of customers paying for a set of cable channels with one set fee

bye weeks the weeks that NFL teams do not play a game; each team gets one bye week per season

credentialed provided with an official pass allowing entry into a private or restricted area

eligibility in this case, the right to continue to play on a college team, granted by both the school and the NCAA

endorsement support and praise offered by a paid spokesperson for a product or service

expansion team a new franchise that starts from scratch

feedback information used to improve something

general managers members of a sports team's front office in charge of building that club's roster

leverage the ability to direct the course of action in a decision

merger to combine into one

perennial occurring or returning every year; annually

protocol in this instance, a pre-planned series of steps or tests undertaken by medical professionals working with players

public relations the process of telling the public about a product, service, or event from the "company" point of view

red zone for the team with possession of the football, the area of the field from the opponents' 20-yard line to the goal line

special teams the kicking game in football: kickoffs, punts, field goals, and extra points

traumatic in medicine, describing an injury that is very significant, resulting in damage to body tissues

INDEX

CREDITS

ABOUT THE AUTHOR

Ted Brock has spent more than four decades as a sportswriter and editor, including eight years on staff at NFL Properties and more than 15 years of writing for the NFL. He has also worked for the *Los Angeles Times*, the *Oakland Tribune*, the *Modesto Bee*, NBCOlympics.com, and MLB.com. Brock also has spent 20 years teaching high school English in northern and southern California, as well as 10 years teaching sportswriting at the University of Southern California.